>>> **e-guidelines** 2

Leicester

Digital cameras in teaching and learning

Phil Hardcastle

promoting adult learning

©2004 National Institute of Adult Continuing Education
(England and Wales)
21 De Montfort Street
Leicester
LE1 7GE

Company registration no. 2603322
Charity registration no. 1002775

NIACE has a broad remit to promote lifelong learning opportunities
for adults. NIACE works to develop increased participation in
education and training, particularly for those who do not have easy
access because of class, gender, age, race, language and culture,
learning difficulties or disabilities, or insufficient financial resources.

You can find NIACE online at **www.niace.org.uk**

Cataloguing in Publication Data
A CIP record of this title is available from the British Library

Designed and typeset by Patrick Armstrong Book Production
Services, London

Printed and bound in the UK by Latimer Trend
ISBN: 1 86201 225 3

Contents

Acknowledgements

NIACE is grateful to the following people for permission to use their pictures:

> Ishbel Marquis and her students at Portsmouth Adult Education Service for the picture of yoga at Wymering;
> Mike North of the Gamelea Countryside Training Trust for the visual diaries picture;
> Elizabeth Whattler and Clare Riordan of Bromley Adult Education Service for the web-based recipe pictures;
> the NIACE staff who 'volunteered' for the photo story: David Ewens, Raksha Mistry and Joanne White;
> Cornwall Art Online of Cornwall Adult Education, for permission to use their photo and text;
> Iffat Shanaz of Camden Adult Education Service for her help and advice.

1

Introduction

Digital cameras have become the normal way to capture pictures for printing, publication and the Web. Digital camera sales in 2003 exceeded film camera sales both in the United States and Europe, where 18 million cameras were bought. As a result both you and your learners will probably be familiar with the use of digital cameras.

Digital cameras have the advantage of immediacy. The pictures taken can be seen immediately on the camera's screen, transferred to a computer, printed out if needed, or used in some other way. There is an instant record of the photographed activity, which can focus learners and teachers on the lesson and stimulate further thought and learning. The use of cameras is a simple and effective way of incorporating e-learning into everyone's classes.

There is also a greater awareness among tutors that not everyone learns in the same way. People who learn best visually or actively will find that the use of digital cameras can help their understanding, while discussing pictures showing situations or processes can help others who benefit from a more verbal approach.

This guide explores the uses of digital cameras in adult and community learning subject areas. It gives examples of good practice when using digital cameras and points to ways in which they can help make learning more effective. It also gives practical instructions in how to take, download and use digital images in educational settings.

2

Key concepts

Learning styles

How do you learn to do something? By and large there was a tendency for older educational systems to assume that everyone learned in the same way, and consequently everyone was taught in the same way. The teacher stood in front of the class and either dictated information or wrote notes on the blackboard to be copied down. It was once described as a system whereby information passed from the teacher to learner without passing through the mind of either.

With increasing research into how people learn it is clear that there are different styles of learning and, while some of us can succeed through being taught in the academic style outlined above, many others need different stimuli to be able to absorb information effectively, and if they are only taught using one style they will not be able to make sense of the subject being taught.

There are several different approaches to describing learning styles, but all agree that visual stimuli can help people to understand processes, concepts and systems. One model that explores how people absorb information categorises people as *auditory*, *visual*, *kinaesthetic* or *tactile* learners. Those who prefer a visual learning style:

> look intently at the teacher's face
> like looking at wall displays, books, etc.
> often recognise words by sight
> use lists to organise their thoughts
> recall information by remembering how it was set out on a page

This is not to say that people have one learning style to the exclusion of all others. Most people will learn in a variety of different ways, depending on the learning content and context. Visual presentations may have more impact on those who prefer a visual learning style, but will also help those whose preference is for other learning styles.

This is because, in any learning process, variety of presentation is important. Learners can get bored easily if only one method of presentation is used. Visual stimuli can provoke reactions among a group of learners and provoke interaction and discussion.

Digital cameras can be used in every subject to enhance understanding because they can provide an immediate visual stimulus to the learning process. Pictures taken of an activity, process or discussion and shown to the class will make learners interact and understand. There are few situations where a digital picture cannot assist the learning process.

The following case studies show a variety of ways in which the camera can be used in different subjects.

3

Cameras in practice

Case studies: the benefits of digital cameras in adult learning

Cornwall Art Online
(http://www.cornwallartonline.com/gallery/albums.php) is an excellent example of the use of digital imagery to showcase the art and design work of tutors and classes.

As well as bringing the work to a wider audience, the site also gives clear and useful advice about how to take digital photographs of artworks, as in the excerpt below.

Taking a good photo of a painting or sculpture that captures something of its quality and character using very simple equipment can be a work of art in itself. It can also be a lot of fun and very rewarding, as many of us discovered. One of the key principles of the Cornwall Art Online project was that we used equipment of a level that most adult

education students could beg, steal or borrow – so no expensive studio lights or digital SLR for us. Daylight bulbs in flexi-necked desk lamps, black material from a well-known out-of-town store for backdrops and little Fuji A203 digital cameras were to be the tools of our trade.

Recording events; visual diaries

The Gamelea Countryside Training Trust uses digital cameras to encourage their learners to record events and create visual diaries. A small multimedia studio and four Sony Mavica cameras are at the heart of this project, and these are being used with great enthusiasm by adults with learning disabilities.

The idea behind the project is to give learners the opportunity to record ideas and events and become involved in the creation of learning resources. The cameras have proved very popular and the learners are keen to see the results on screen. The digital activities have had a noticeable impact on the learners' confidence and generated a lot of discussion and group interaction.

Gamelea is situated on a working farm and learning often focuses on the farm's activities. This environment provides a great visual stimulus and tutors are also able to create visual materials that link directly to the learners' experiences.

Exciting farm events like the recent arrival of two llamas provided an ideal opportunity for Shirley, Geoff, Kay and Olive to use their newly acquired photography skills to record the occasion. Elizabeth Hill, the Centre Manager, is sure this project will continue to have a real impact on the way resources are developed and the way learners record and develop ideas.

Technical illustration example

Cookery in Bromley

Bromley Adult Education Service uses digital photography to provide illustrations for cookery courses. The photos illustrate the techniques, methods and materials needed for a variety of recipes. The pictures and recipes have been put together in Word and then set up in Web pages using the CourseGenie program. This has the advantage of providing easy navigation through the recipes and easy distribution of the materials.

Overview of the Web-based recipes produced by Bromley Adult Education Service

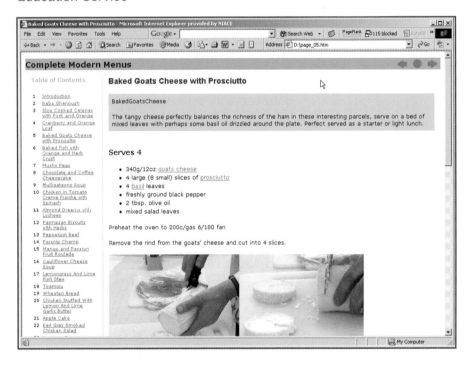

Detail from one of the recipes, showing the use of pictures

Place a slice of goat's cheese on top and season with black pepper. Wrap up neatly in the prosciutto.

Remove the rind from the goat's cheese and cut into 4 slices.

Lay out the prosciutto and place a basil leaf in the centre of each piece.

Preheat the oven to 200°C/Gas 6/180° fan

Health and fitness example

Yoga at Wymering

Here the yoga teacher has used digital photography to take photographs of her learners in order to illustrate good posture and position. They have then been imported into a PowerPoint presentation which can be used individually by students to revise or to catch up on things they have missed, or by the teacher as a teaching aid.

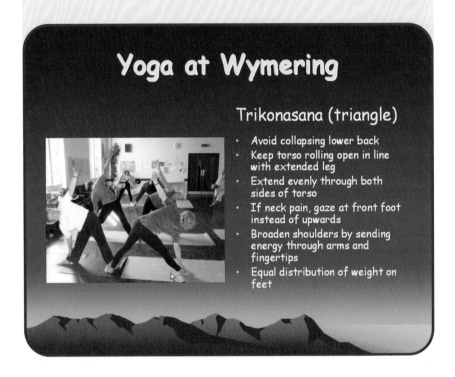

4

Working with the camera

Digital cameras vary slightly in their design. The controls may be in different places and the way in which the camera is operated will vary according to the particular make. However, the basic operations are very similar. We'll now describe the basic functions of any camera. (For details on using specific cameras, consult your camera instruction booklet.)

The process

1   Taking pictures
2   Reviewing pictures
3   Deleting unwanted pictures
4   Transferring the images to a computer
5   Printing or using the images

Changing the camera mode

Cameras can have three basic modes:

a   Taking a picture
b   Reviewing pictures
c   Changing settings

There may be a fourth mode, for taking short video clips.

These modes can be selected using the camera controls, which will differ according to the make of camera. The pictures below show two types of camera control.

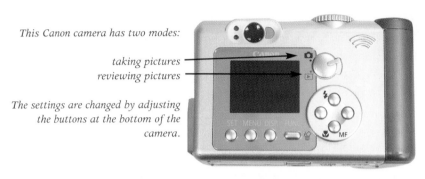

This Canon camera has two modes:

taking pictures
reviewing pictures

The settings are changed by adjusting
the buttons at the bottom of the
camera.

This Sony camera has four modes:

reviewing pictures
taking pictures
video clips
settings

Taking pictures

Most digital cameras can be used as 'point-and-click' devices. Turn
the camera on, select 'camera' (the mode for taking pictures), look at
the image through the viewfinder or screen at the back of the camera
and press the shutter button. The screen at the back of the camera
will display, for a few seconds, the picture you have taken. When
using a camera in class this gives you a chance to decide quickly if
the picture is good enough to use or whether you need to take a
second shot.

Many cameras have a zoom lens which is usually operated by a
control near the shutter button.

Reviewing pictures

Change the camera mode to 'review' and use the camera controls to
move through the pictures you have taken. Although the screen is
small you will be able to see which photographs need deleting and

which can be saved. On some cameras it is also possible to zoom in on the image in the rear screen of the camera. Where your photograph includes images of learners themselves this is a point at which they can be given the opportunity to approve or reject images taken of them.

Deleting unwanted pictures

You can delete pictures from the camera memory by using a dedicated button or by using the camera's menu system. Alternatively you can delete them after opening up the camera drive in 'My Computer'.

Transferring the images to a computer

There are a number of ways of doing this, depending on your equipment and your computer's operating system. If you are doing this during a teaching session it is important to be familiar with the particular method available to you.

Using a card reader

A card reader is a device that can be connected to a computer or can be already built in. Take the camera memory card out of the camera and place it in the card reader. The computer can now see the memory card as a disk drive. Open up 'My Computer' to see the memory card appear as an extra drive. You can then copy the pictures from this drive to the hard drive of the computer – typically into the 'My Pictures' area of 'My Documents'.

Card reader with compact flash-card inserted. The lead connects to the USB port of the computer.

Many newer desktop computers may have built-in card readers. These look like small floppy drives. Laptop computers can have a card reader inserted into the PCMCIA slot in their side.

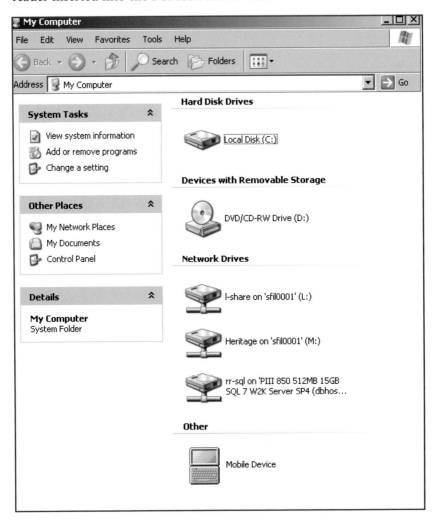

The 'My Computer' window before the insertion of the card reader.

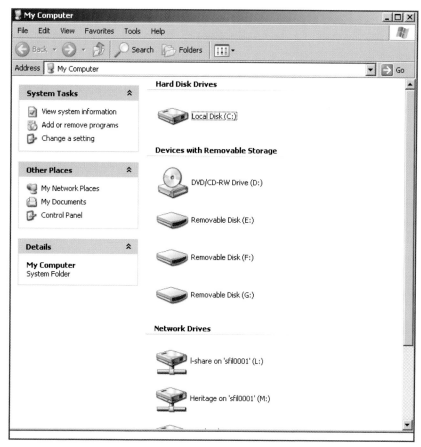

The 'My Computer' window after the insertion of the card reader.

Notice the extra drives E, F and G. This is because there are three slots in the card reader for three types of card.

To see the pictures on the card, double-click on the drive corresponding to the slot in which the card was inserted. Double-click on the DCIM folder ('Digital Camera Images') to get to the images.

Connecting the camera directly to a computer

Most cameras come with a lead which connects the camera to the computer's USB port. Before connecting the lead you may need to install software called 'drivers' onto the computer from the CD which came with the camera. Once the drivers have been installed, connect the camera to the computer with the lead supplied. This goes from the camera to a USB port on the computer.

The computer should then recognise the camera as a disk drive in 'My Computer'. You can then drag picture files from this drive to the 'My Pictures' folder in 'My Documents'. The process is very similar to that outlined for the card reader above.

Most cameras also come with software to help the transfer process. The quality of this software is variable – in most cases it may be easier to transfer the pictures using the methods outlined above. However, the software will normally also have some basic image-editing facilities which may be useful – for example, it may help you to remove red-eye from pictures or to lighten or darken the image.

Printing or using the images

Once they have been transferred to a computer, images can be printed out directly to a printer, or can be inserted into text documents where they might be used in worksheets and for evidence in students' portfolios. They can also be used in electronic resources such as Web pages and presentations, or sent as attachments via email – in this case you will need to change the size of the pictures (see below).

Some specially designed inkjet printers have card readers which will read the card memory of the printer and print out the images. Others can be connected directly to the printer for this purpose.

Camera memory cards can be taken to photo-processing shops where the images can be printed off or archived onto CD-ROM. This can also be arranged via the Internet, although because of the large amount of data being transferred you should only attempt this if you have a good broadband connection.

A practical guide to the digital camera

Different makes of camera are designed differently, but all will have the following elements.

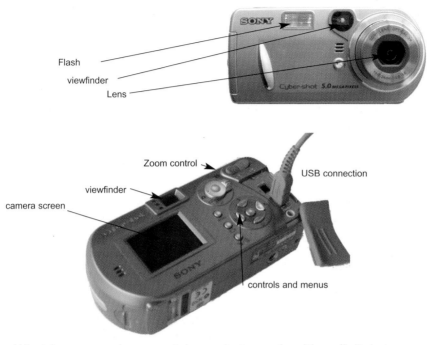

Flash

viewfinder

Lens

Zoom control

USB connection

viewfinder

camera screen

controls and menus

What happens when you take a photograph with a digital camera?

Instead of being recorded on light-sensitive film the image is recorded onto a light-sensitive chip, which captures the image and saves it to the memory of the camera. The camera memory will hold the image until it is deleted using the camera controls, or by a computer when the two are connected.

Response time

Some cameras have a faster response time when the shutter is pressed. If a camera has a slow response time, then any movement of the camera will make the picture blurred. Some digital cameras cannot take a series of pictures quickly, and there is a delay after the shutter is pressed while the image is saved to the camera's memory. If you want to take pictures of fast-moving action in, for example, a sports or dance class, a good response time is important.

Video clips

Many cameras will take short video clips, typically lasting about half a minute. These have an obvious use in sport, design and crafts areas to illustrate techniques or to record acquired skills.

Memory cards

There are several different types of memory card – each camera normally takes only one type. Memory cards come in different sizes, measured in megabytes. The larger the card in megabytes, the more pictures it will store.

Megapixels and resolution

A pixel is the basic building block of a digital image. Each pixel has information about the brightness and colour of that small part of the image. The more pixels recorded by a camera's light-sensitive device the more detail is stored by the camera. Think of a one-inch square with 16 pixels in it – the information recorded will not be very detailed and will be blocky and fuzzy. If you now imagine that same one-inch square with 128 pixels in it, you can see that much more detail can be recorded because there are 128 sets of information about brightness and colour in that same area.

Most consumer cameras are sold as 3-, 4-, 5- or 6-megapixel cameras. Professional models will go even higher, with 8, 10 or 14 megapixels (the mega stands for one million pixels). A high mega-pixel count can also be referred to as a higher picture resolution, because the increased number of pixels resolves more detail.

For most purposes in education a 3- or 4-megapixel camera will be sufficient. If, however, you need large-format images, i.e. prints of A4 size or larger, then it is worth considering buying a camera with 5 or 6 megapixels. If photographs are to be used in printed brochures then a large format is usually needed.

Until recently the number of megapixels a camera could capture was used to indicate the quality of the camera – the more megapixels, the better the quality. This is no longer necessarily the case, because the other major factor is the quality of the lens system used in the camera. Cameras with cheap plastic lenses will produce poorer pictures than those with good quality glass lenses made by an established manufacturer, e.g. Zeiss or Canon.

5

Working with digital images

Taking good pictures

There is more to taking pictures than knowing how to operate the
camera. A good picture will have interest and impact. Usually, when
taking pictures of people, this means getting close to the subject.
Good, strong images with contrast between the foreground and
background will focus student interest and provoke an enthusiastic
response.

Have a look at this website for some clear advice about composing
pictures:
http://www.fotofinish.com/resources/centers/photo/takingpictures.htm

Changing the size of pictures

It is likely that the picture taken in the camera is not the size that you
need for your particular teaching resource, so you will need to change
its size. For example, when sending a picture by email it is usually a
good idea to reduce the size of the picture. This can be done with the
software which comes with the camera or with some simple software
which comes with Windows, Microsoft Photo Editor.Typically this is
done through the Image>Resize menu as shown below, which uses
Photo Editor. Other image editors, e.g. Photoshop or Paintshop Pro,
do the same thing in much the same way.

Insert
Resize
selected

This will reduce the file size of the picture, reflecting a reduction in its resolution, enabling it to be sent easily via email.

To check the disk space taken up by the picture, open 'My Documents' and open the folder where the picture is kept. Right-click on the picture file and select 'Properties'.

current size of picture

picture size changed

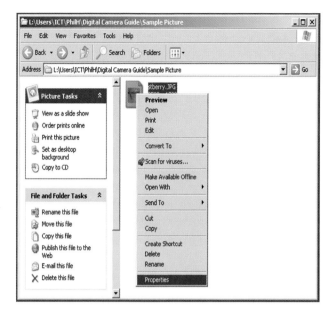

*right-click on the
picture file and
select 'Properties'.*

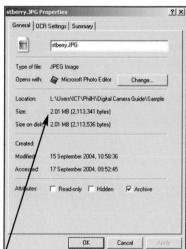

*Properties box showing the size before
editing: 2.01Mb. This would take some
time to send by email or download
from the Web, especially with a slow,
dial-up connection.*

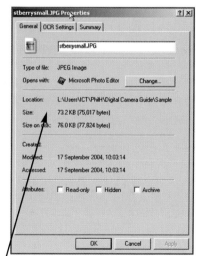

*The Properties box showing the size after
editing: 73.2kb. This is much smaller and can
be used as a Web picture or sent by email.*

19

Bear in mind that the person receiving the picture cannot reverse this process. You can enlarge pictures which have been reduced in size, but the quality of the image, its sharpness, will be poorer than the original.

This is true of any attempt to enlarge pictures. Beyond a certain point the picture will begin to lose sharpness as the pixels are pulled further apart and the definition of the image begins to suffer.

Editing copies of images

When editing a picture it is a good idea to start by clicking on 'File > Save As' and save the picture under another name. This prevents your image-editing experiments overwriting a crucial image. It is always a good idea to edit a copy of the picture rather than the original.

Importing pictures into Word, PowerPoint or a desktop publishing program such as Publisher

Pictures can be brought into Word, Publisher or any other program to create teaching resources. Learners can also use pictures as part of the recording of their work. All Microsoft Office programs work in much the same way as the example below – these instructions are for Word, PowerPoint and Publisher, but other programs operate in a similar way.

Click Insert > Picture > From File

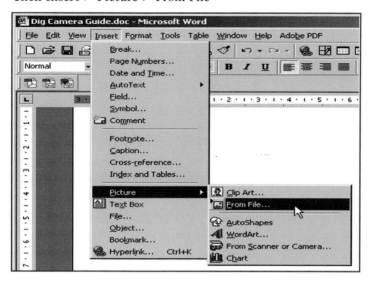

Select the file to be inserted and click 'Insert'.

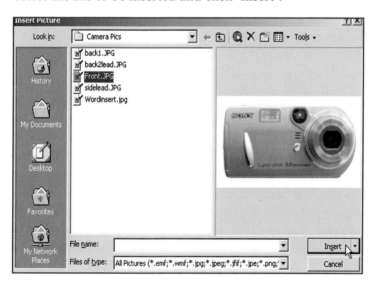

The picture will now be placed into your document.

Dragging pictures and wrapping text around the picture

The picture can then be placed more accurately in the document as follows:

This picture bar will be displayed when the picture is selected in the document.

To drag the picture around the document, click on the Word Wrap icon in the picture bar. Select one of the options from the drop-down menu. 'Square' is the most frequently used option.

This will have two effects. First, you will be able to click on the picture and drag it around the document. Secondly, text will now wrap around the picture rather than appearing above and below the picture. This can be very important to ensure that images are placed in exactly the right place in handouts so that they complement the text accurately.

Resizing pictures in Word, PowerPoint and Publisher

Click on the picture to make it editable.

Click on one of the control points in the corner of the picture. The cursor will change to a double-headed arrow. Now drag this diagonally inwards (or outwards) to decrease or increase the size. Note that a corner control point should be used to avoid distorting the picture.

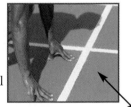

Direction of drag

It can happen that the picture jumps back to its original size. To overcome this, click on the picture and first select a text-wrap option before trying again to resize the picture.

It is also worth noting that decreasing the area of the picture in this way has no effect on the size in terms of the disk space taken up by the picture. To reduce the picture in this way you will need a picture editor such as Microsoft Photo Editor.

Inserting pictures into Hot Potatoes

Hot Potatoes is a program which allows tutors to develop quizzes, crosswords and other Web-based interactive learning modules. It is simple to operate and generates Web pages which can be saved and used on any computer.

Pictures for Web pages need to be kept small for two reasons: first to ensure they download quickly on the Internet, and secondly so that they are the correct size for the Web page. Hot Potatoes can import pictures, and Version 6 of the program has an editor which can be used to adjust them to the correct size.

The example shown is a matching exercise, where the correct French words are matched with a picture of the object.

In the form shown the pictures are added to the boxes on the left using Insert>Picture>Picture from local file.

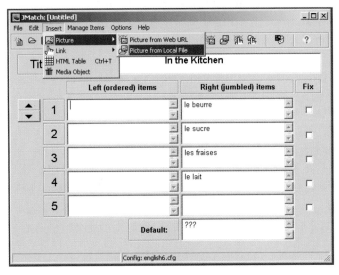

The Hot Potatoes editor opens the picture.

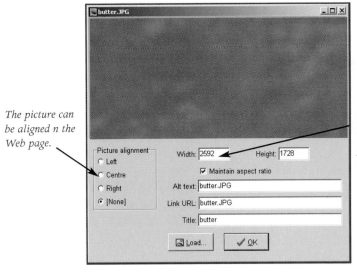

The picture can be aligned n the Web page.

The size of the picture in pixels can be changed.

Editor, showing the picture reduced in size. Note the significant change in width. Note also that this does not reduce the disk space taken up by the picture, just the dimensions of the picture on the Web page. It may still be a good idea to reduce the size in megabytes, as outlined earlier in the section reducing the size of pictures.

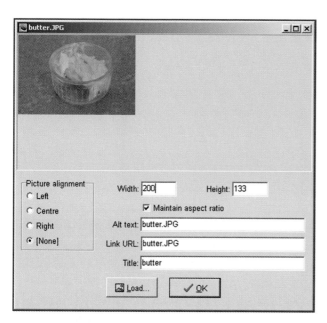

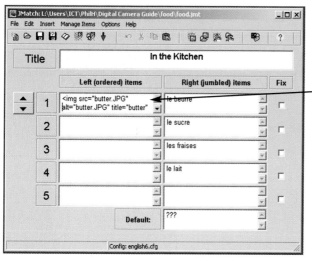

Hot Potatoes then puts text into the original form, describing where the picture is and how big it is.

When Hot Potatoes creates the finished Web page for the learner the pictures are the correct size for the Web page. The learner can then drag the text boxes across to the appropriate picture.

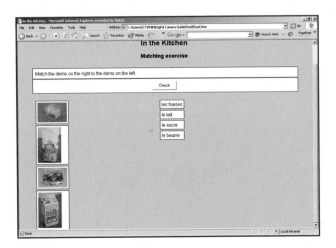

Experimenting and developing

This guide touches on some of the ways in which digital cameras can be used in the teaching and learning process. However, digital cameras have only been in use in education for a relatively short time, which means that you and your learners can continually be thinking of new ways of employing cameras and pictures to enhance their classroom experience.

Possible developments might include:

> the use of multimedia mobile phones to take pictures and send them back to base

> cameras being given to students for them to record their own progress in visual media

> simple photo stories shot to stimulate student interaction, e.g. in a language class

> the use of dictation machines with cameras to record students' progress, or used by students to put together an audiovisual diary of their learning

Creating a photo story

The example below shows a simple photo story, shot in 15 minutes. It could be used to stimulate discussion or to provide the outline of a story. Alternatively, captions or speech bubbles could be created and the learner could drag them to the appropriate parts of the story.

Sharing pictures

Tutors often find it useful to share resources, and digital images are no exception. The National Learning Network has funded an online image library where tutors can upload pictures for others to use, and download pictures, for use in education. The library can be found at: www.aclearn.net.

6

Conclusion

This guide shows how digital photography can be used very effectively when teaching adults in all subjects. Tutors can use digital images to add relevant and motivating images to teaching resources and learners can use images as part of their coursework. Both tutors and learners can also use digital cameras to record their progress and achievement.

As digital cameras become more widely used we must not lose the opportunity to harness this technology to improve the quality of teaching and learning for adults. The resources are becoming available, so the message is: get out and have a go!

7
Glossary

Aperture	The opening in the camera lens which allows light to enter and reach the light-sensitive element
Card reader	A device for reading camera memory cards
Download	The process of transferring images from a camera to a computer
e-learning	The use of technology to enhance the teaching and learning process
Image editor	A program on a computer which allows the user to edit digital photographs
JPEG	A standard for compressing photographs so that they take up less space on a disk or in the memory, while retaining as much quality as possible
LCD	Liquid crystal display; the small screen at the rear of the camera
Learning styles	The different methods by which people prefer to absorb information
Lens	This focuses the image onto the light-sensitive device
Megabytes	A measurement of the size of a computer hard disk in millions of bytes
Megapixels	A measurement of how many pixels there are in pictures taken with a camera *see also* **Pixel**
Memory	Temporary storage in a computer or a camera for storing information
Memory card	The card in a camera which is the temporary store for the images

Pixel	A picture element, the smallest element of a picture. There will be thousands or millions of these in any one picture
PowerPoint	A program for displaying presentations which may include text, pictures or video. Part of the Microsoft Office suite of programs
Resolution	The higher the number of pixels in an image the greater the resolution of the camera
Shutter	A mechanical device in the camera which opens briefly to let light through the aperture onto the light-sensitive element
SLR	Single Lens Reflex camera. The viewfinder looks through the lens of the camera to compose the picture
USB connection	The lead connecting the camera to the computer's USB port
Viewfinder	The glass viewer by which the user sees the scene to be photographed
Zoom	A zoom lens can bring the subject of the photograph closer. Optical zoom lenses will give better results than digital zoom

There are many digital photography glossaries on the Web – here are two of them. More can be found by typing *digital photography glossary* into a search engine such as Google or Yahoo.

http://www.microsoft.com/windowsxp/using/digitalphotography/glossary/default.mspx

http://support.radioshack.com/support_tutorials/audio_video/digvid-glossary.htm

8

Useful websites

Composing good pictures
http://www.fotofinish.com/resources/centers/photo/takingpictures.htm

Digital cameras in education
http://members.ozemail.com.au/~cumulus/digcam.htm#TOP

Going Digital in the Classroom – a list of ideas for using digital cameras in education
http://www.forsyth.k12.ga.us/sbeck/digital/goingdigital.htm

Short online courses in using digital cameras
http://www.shortcourses.com/

Digital cameras in education
http://www.kn.sbc.com/wired/fil/pages/listdigitalst2.html

A review of the use of digital cameras in education, with some useful ideas and links
http://www.aclearn.net/technical/hardware/cameras/

Digital Photography Review – an online guide to new cameras and kit
http://www.dpreview.com/

Agfa guide to Digital Photography
http://www.agfanet.com/en/cafe/photocourse/digicourse/lesson1/cont_index.php3

Digicaminfo – lots of links to lots of sites
http://www.digicaminfo.com/links.htm

Kodak's Digital Learning Centre
http://www.kodak.com/US/en/digital/dlc/

How Stuff Works – the digital camera
http://www.howstuffworks.com/digital-camera1.htm

Photoshop tutorials
http://myjanee.home.insightbb.com/tutorials.htm

Common mistakes
http://www.microsoft.com/windowsxp/using/digitalphotography/thebigpicture/top10.mspx

Tutorials for Adobe products
http://www.adobe.com/education/training/main.html

How to email digital photos
http://photos.msn.com (select the link to emailing photos)

9
Further reading

Rapid developments in digital camera technology mean that books on digital cameras tend to go out of date fairly rapidly, so treat this list with some caution. There are lots of books about digital photography editing using programs such as Adobe Photoshop. This list concentrates on books which describe using the camera.

Complete Guide to Digital Photography (with CD-ROM), Michael Freeman, Thames & Hudson, 2003, ISBN 0500542775.

Digital Photography and Computing for the Older Generation, Jim Gatenby, Babani, 2003, ISBN 0859346021.

Digital Photography Basics, Les Meehan, Collins & Brown, 2003, ISBN 1843400421.

Digital Photography for Dummies, Julie Adair-King, John Wiley, 2002, ISBN 0764516647.

Digital Photography Handbook, Tom Ang, Dorling Kindersley, 2004, ISBN 0756603463

Digital Photography in Easy Steps, Nick Vandone, Computer Step, 2003, ISBN 1840781998.

Digital Photography Special Effects, Michael Freeman, Watson-Guptill, 2003, ISBN 0817438254.

Digital Photography Step by Step, Jerry Glenwright, HarperCollins, 2003, ISBN 0007146833.

The Digital Photography Workbook, Simon Joinson, Trafalgar Square, 2002, ISBN 1570762325.

Digital Photography: An Introduction, Tom Ang, Dorling Kindersley, 2003, ISBN 1405302356.

How to Do Everything with Your Digital Camera, Dave Johnson, McGraw-Hill Osborne Media; 3rd edition 2003, ISBN 007 22 3081 9.

Real World Digital Photography, Tim Grey *et al.*, Peachpit Press, 2003, ISBN 0321223721.

Shooting Digital: Pro Tips for Taking Great Pictures with Your Digital Camera, Mikkel Aaland, Sybex International, 2003, ISBN: 0782141048.

(The Complete Beginner's Guide to) Using a Digital Camera for the First Time, Bill Hall, Management Books, 2003, ISBN 1852524308.